HAPPY BIRTH

CW00820438

TO

....

WITH LOVE FROM   ·

....

And Oscar

HAPPY BIRTHDAY—LOVE . . .

Complete Series

Jane Austen

Joan Crawford

Bette Davis

Liam Gallagher

Audrey Hepburn

John Lennon

Bob Marley

Marilyn Monroe

Michelle Obama

Jackie Kennedy Onassis

Elvis Presley

Keith Richards

Frank Sinatra

Elizabeth Taylor

Oscar Wilde

HAPPY BIRTHDAY

Love, Oscar

ON YOUR SPECIAL DAY

ENJOY THE WIT AND WISDOM OF

OSCAR WILDE

BELOVED GENTLEMAN OF LETTERS

Edited by Jade Riley

CELEBRATION BOOKS

THIS IS A CELEBRATION BOOK

Published by Celebration Books 2023
Celebration Books is an imprint of Dean Street Press

Text & Design Copyright © 2023 Celebration Books

All Rights Reserved. No part of this publication may be reproduced, stored in or transmitted in any form or by any means without the written permission of the copyright owner and the publisher of this book.

Cover by DSP

ISBN 978 1 915393 80 7

www.deanstreetpress.co.uk

HAPPY BIRTHDAY—LOVE, OSCAR

Oscar Wilde was born on October 16, 1854
in Dublin, Ireland, the son of minor, Anglo-Irish
aristocracy in possession of distinct intellectual
tastes. Educated at first by governesses, he easily
mastered French and German as a child. Labeled
a prodigy, he won scholarships and honors to
Trinity College and Oxford University. There, Wilde
quickly became enmeshed with the Aesthetic and
Decadent movements alongside his reading of "the
Greats" as classical studies were known. Wilde's
flamboyant nature and curiosity saw him write
poetry, dabble in Catholicism and Freemasonry
and basically proclaim his genius to all who all

knew him. A favorite example of this being "I find it harder and harder every day to live up to my blue china." Indeed this is a fine start for a man whose last words are quoted as being "My wallpaper and I are fighting a duel to the death. One of us has got to go".

The life he led between these two epigrams was a mixture of creative abandon and hard work. His first play *Salome*, written in French while in Paris, was produced to critical acclaim and borrowed by Strauss for the opera. He then tackled the jobs of editing a woman's magazine, worked as an art critic, and published two collections of children's stories. Ever hungry for adventure, he toured America to public acclaim, staying eight months longer than planned. Although sometimes a pioneering celebrity, famous for being famous, his decadent novel, *The Picture of Dorian Gray*, enjoyed a success which proved Wilde worthy of his renown. His next play, *Lady Windermere's Fan*, enjoyed such success that he became the most important playwright of his age. His subsequent plays, *A Woman of No Importance*, *An Ideal Husband* and The Importance of Being Earnest, now classics of the English theater, are further proof that Wilde's humor and wisdom continue to transcend his epoch.

So, open a bottle of champagne, and toast yourself in the excellent company of that supreme wordsmith, Oscar Wilde.

oscar wilde

I don't want
to go to heaven.
None of my
friends are there.

I am so clever that sometimes I don't understand a single word of what I am saying.

One should
always play
fairly when one
has the winning
cards.

Education is an admirable thing, but it is well to remember from time to time that nothing that is worth knowing can be taught.

Questions are
never indiscreet,
answers
sometimes are.

"

Hatred is blind, as well as love.

"

When one is in love, one always begins by deceiving one's self, and one always ends by deceiving others. That is what the world calls a romance.

When I was young I thought that money was the most important thing in life; now that I am old I know that it is.

It is absurd to divide people into good and bad. People are either charming or tedious.

No woman should ever be quite accurate about her age. It looks so calculating.

Selfishness is not living as one wishes to live, it is asking others to live as one wishes to live.

I have the
simplest tastes.
I am always
satisfied with
the best.

Life is never fair, and perhaps it is a good thing for most of us that it is not.

Life imitates
art far more
than art
imitates Life.

Never love
anyone who
treats you like
you're ordinary.

I can resist
anything
except
temptation.

Laughter is not at all a bad beginning for a friendship, and it is far the best ending for one.

When a man has
once loved a woman
he will do anything for
her except continue
to love her.

One can survive everything, nowadays, except death, and live down everything except a good reputation.

"

To expect the
unexpected
shows a thoroughly
modern intellect.

Man is a rational animal who always loses his temper when he is called upon to act in accordance with the dictates of reason.

Anybody can sympathize with the sufferings of a friend, but it requires a very fine nature to sympathize with a friend's success.

The only difference between the saint and the sinner is that every saint has a past, and every sinner has a future.

Experience is one thing you can't get for nothing.

A man who
does not think
for himself does
not think at all.

It is better to have a permanent income than to be fascinating.

Whenever people agree with me I always feel I must be wrong.

The true mystery
of the world is
the visible, not
the invisible.

Beauty is the only thing
that time cannot harm.
Philosophies fall away like
sand, creeds follow one
another, but what is beautiful
is a joy for all seasons, a
possession for all eternity.

Our ambition should be to rule ourselves, the true kingdom for each one of us; and true progress is to know more, and be more, and to do more.

The good ended
happily, and the
bad unhappily.
That is what fiction
means.

Society often
forgives the
criminal; it never
forgives the
dreamer.

Every portrait that is painted with feeling is a portrait of the artist, not of the sitter.

In this world there are only two tragedies. One is not getting what one wants, and the other is getting it.

Morality is simply the attitude we adopt towards people we personally dislike.

The nicest feeling in the world is to do a good deed anonymously— and have somebody find out.

A thing is not
necessarily true
because a man
dies for it.

A good friend
will always
stab you in the
front.

To live is the rarest
thing in the world.
Most people exist,
that is all.

If one cannot enjoy
reading a book over
and over again,
there is no use in
reading it at all.

The truth is
rarely pure
and never
simple.

The books that the world calls immoral are books that show the world its own shame.

You can never
be overdressed
or over-
educated.

The critic has
to educate the
public; the artist
has to educate
the critic.

One of the many lessons that one learns in prison is, that things are what they are and will be what they will be.

If you pretend to be good, the world takes you very seriously. If you pretend to be bad, it doesn't. Such is the astounding stupidity of optimism.

If you want to tell people the truth, make them laugh, otherwise, they'll kill you.

Always forgive
your enemies;
nothing annoys
them so much.

Some cause
happiness
wherever they go;
others whenever
they go.

When the gods
wish to punish
us, they answer
our prayers.

Most people die of a sort
of creeping common
sense, and discover when
it is too late that the only
things one never regrets
are one's mistakes.

After a good dinner one can forgive anybody, even one's own relatives.

Ordinary riches can be stolen; real riches cannot. In your soul are infinitely precious things that cannot be taken from you.

What is a cynic? A man who knows the price of everything and the value of nothing.

We live in an age
when unnecessary
things are our only
necessities.

A man's face is his autobiography. A woman's face is her work of fiction.

I choose my friends for their good looks, my acquaintances for their good characters, and my enemies for their intellects. A man cannot be too careful in the choice of his enemies.

Humanity takes itself too seriously. It is the world's original sin. If the cave-man had known how to laugh, History would have been different.

A little sincerity is a
dangerous thing,
and a great deal of
it is absolutely fatal.

Most people are other people. Their thoughts are someone else's opinions, their lives a mimicry, their passions a quotation.

Anyone who lives within their means suffers from a lack of imagination.

A man who can dominate a London dinner-table can dominate the world.

The only way
to get rid of
temptation is to
yield to it.

It takes great deal of courage to see the world in all its tainted glory, and still to love it.

The public is wonderfully tolerant. It forgives everything except genius.

They've promised that dreams can come true—but forgot to mention that nightmares are dreams, too.

When I am in trouble, eating is the only thing that consoles me. Indeed, when I am in really great trouble, as anyone who knows me intimately will tell you, I refuse everything except food and drink.

Thirty-five is a very attractive age. London society is full of women of the very highest birth who have, of their own free choice, remained thirty-five for years.

One should never trust
a woman who tells one
her real age. A woman
who would tell one that
would tell one anything.

The old believe
everything, the
middle-aged suspect
everything, the young
know everything.

To love oneself
is the beginning
of a lifelong
romance.

I think God, in
creating man,
somewhat
overestimated
his ability.

Man can believe
the impossible,
but man can
never believe the
improbable.

There is no necessity to separate the monarch from the mob; all authority is equally bad.

The moment
you think you
understand a
great work of art,
it's dead for you.

Those whom
the gods love
grow young.

An animal is as
loving, caring,
and kind to
her children as
we are.

The well bred
contradict other
people. The
wise contradict
themselves.

Experience is merely the name men gave to their mistakes.

I always pass on
good advice. It is the
only thing to do with
it. It is never of any
use to oneself.

A bore is someone who deprives you of solitude without providing you with company.

To get back my youth
I would do anything in
the world, except take
exercise, get up early,
or be respectable.

There is only one thing in the world worse than being talked about, and that is not being talked about.

I can't stand
people that do
not take food
seriously.

Keep love in your heart. A life without it is like a sunless garden when the flowers are dead.

One's real life is
so often the life
that one does
not lead.

oscar wilde

ABOUT THE EDITOR

JADE Riley is a writer whose interests include old movies, art history, vintage fashion and books, books, books.

Her dream is to move to London, to write like Virginia Woolf, and to meet a man like Mr. Darcy, who owns a vacation home in Greece.

Printed in Great Britain
by Amazon

30496448R00057